GULF IN IRELAND

TIGER BOOKS INTERNATIONAL
LONDON

3058
This edition published in 1993 by
Tiger Books International PLC, London
© 1993 CLB Publishing,
Godalming, Surrey
Printed and bound in Italy by New Interlitho
1-85501-345-2

day. The clubhouse itself is superbly appointed with full meals available in the dining room, and filling bar snacks in the lounge.

Shandon Park Golf Club lies north of Belfast with a course of 6249 yards. This

is the home of the old Ulster Open Championship and here, from the course, players have a good view of Stormont Castle on the hill – this was once the seat of government in the province. This is a challenging course which is well worth visiting. Visitors are welcome on any day of the week except Saturdays and will find the green fees very reasonable.

Belvoir Park lies three miles south of Belfast in rolling parkland and was founded in 1927. It was laid out by Harry Colt – the man who designed Sunningdale and many other great courses – using teams of horses and hand ploughs. In 1949, it hosted the Irish Open won by Harry Bradshaw who earlier that year had missed out in the Open Championship itself when his ball came to rest in a broken bottle!

More recently, Belvoir Park has played host to the WPGA and the women professionals admired the course. From the back tees, it measures an impressive 6276 yards with most of the holes wending their way through mature and

The 9th hole at Royal County Down, which plays towards the clubhouse and the beautiful Mountains of Mourne which are an ever-present feature

majestic trees. Visitors are nearly always welcome, and, again, green fees are low.

Balmoral Golf Club, with its flat parkland course, is close to the centre of Belfast. Young trees line the fairways of this course and the clubhouse has a special Fred Daly corner as the former British Open champion has been a regular there for many years. Green fees are modest and meals are usually available in the clubhouse.

Dunmurry Golf Club's new course is only a few miles away. At 5832 yards with an SSS of 68, it is an impressive layout despite its youthfulness, and a good test of golfing skills. However, it probably needs just a little more time to mature. On the adjoining land is the Lady Dixon Park, home of the International Rose Trials, so in the summer months a wonderful fragrance pervades the course.

Malone Golf Club is four miles south of the city centre. The attractive course winds its way round a series of trout lakes, and the first hole goes down almost to the River Lagan's edge. During its history, the club has had a number of changes of site, the current one having been in use since 1962. In

1966 a further nine holes were opened, leading to some adjustment to the original layout, but the only change since then has been to the short par-3 15th to bring in more of the trout lake. This was done in 1984, and since then the hole, even at a mere 147 yards, has been regarded as a card wrecker, so be warned! You can play on any days except Tuesdays and Saturdays.

Royal Belfast, surprisingly, is classed as being in County Down rather than in the city itself. A real beauty of a course, it has a stiff, uphill opening hole with the 8th, 9th, 10th and 11th following the shoreline of the picturesque Belfast Lough. Many golfers regard the 10th as the best hole out of the 18. This is a little honey of 312 yards to a plateau fairway and the green beyond, with perils awaiting you on the left and an extremely difficult target to hit from the right.

Royal Belfast Golf Club is the oldest in Ireland having celebrated its centenary in 1981. The course is excellent and any visitor who misses it out of his itinerary is depriving himself of a rare treat. However, letters of introduction are necessary, and one from your own Club Secretary will probably be suf-

The clubhouse, at Royal County Down, is welcoming after playing a course which has been rated among the world's best

ficient. Moreover, green fees are very modest, making it excellent value for money and worth visiting.

Fortwilliam Golf Club, established in 1903, is three miles north of Belfast with a fairly short course of 5275 yards. **Knockbracken** with its floodlit driving range lies south-east of the city, and there are nine-hole courses at **Ormeau, Gilnahirk** and **Cliftonville.**

Knock Golf Club is further east with a parkland course set in 100 acres. Although there is no rough, there are plenty of well-established trees and 75 bunkers – probably more than any other course in Ireland. It is tight but well-manicured with a par of 69.

Royal County Down golf course is one of the best three or four courses to be found anywhere in the British Isles. To get there, travel south from Belfast on the A24 or A21. The roads link at Ballynahinch where you take the A24 and then the A2 to Newcastle. This course is an old-fashioned links at its very best – grandeur supreme with huge sand dunes. The course is overlooked by the majestic Mountains of Mourne which really do sweep down right to the edge of the sea.

Warrenpoint, the home club of Ronan Rafferty, lies further south. This club has a happy, friendly atmosphere and the members are very welcoming to visitors. The course is sited within view of southern Ireland from which it is separated by Carlingford Lough which extends to the border town of Newry, about five miles away.

A short par-4 but the 5th green at Royal Portrush is dangerously close to the sea and needed protection from it

Ardglass, Downpatrick and **Bright Castle** golf courses are further back out of Newcastle along the A2 and A25. Ardglass, set on the rocks beside the sea, is well worth visiting. Look out especially for the 2nd and 11th holes, both par-3's by the water's edge.

Kirkistown Castle Golf Club is on the Ards Peninsula. To reach it, you have to cross on the little ferry at Strangford and motor up the A20. The journey is worth it and you will be well rewarded. The legendary James Braid carried out the bunkering on the then newly laid out course, and sighed, "Ah, if only I had this within 50 miles of London".

The course has two distinct loops of nine holes starting and finishing at the clubhouse, and the whole atmosphere of club and course is what real golf in Northern Ireland is all about. It is golf right down to the basics, and how the members love it! Visitors pay a very modest fee to sample the delights of the 'Tower,' the 'Quarry' and the 'Moat,' to name but three of the interesting holes. The whole course overlooks the Irish Sea and is located towards the bottom of the Ards Peninsula on the outskirts of the little town of Cloughey.

Royal Portrush and its fabulous links course is only an hour or so from Belfast. Situated on the beautiful scenic Causeway Coast it is almost within spitting distance of three other great links courses – those at Portstewart, Castlerock and Ballycastle. You can play all four courses and stay at any number of delightful hotels in the little resorts and fishing villages. The Causeway Coast gets its name from the spectacular and awe-inspiring Giant's Causeway which looks like gigantic boulders and sculptured stone pillars rising out of the sea. You will hear this described as a geological freak or as the work of the giant Finn McCool, who threw a clod of earth at a fleeing enemy and where it landed in the sea became the Isle of Man! McCool then fell in love with a lady giant on the Hebridean Island of Staffa and started to build the Giant's Causeway as a road to fetch her back across the sea. It is worth breaking off from your golf to go and visit this amazing stone monument.

Royal Portrush is along the coastal road from the Giant's Causeway past the burned-out ruins of Dunluce Castle. It is the only course in Ireland to have hosted the Open Championship – in 1951 when the winner was Max Faulkner. It still remains as one of the best links courses in the world.

Bernard Darwin, the doyen of golf writers, wrote in *The Times* of July 3rd 1951: 'It is a truly magnificent course and Mr H.S. Colt who designed it in its present form, has thereby built himself a monument more enduring than brass. The course does not disdain the spectacular, such as the one-shot hole called "Calamity Corner" with its terrifying sandy cliffs and its gadarene descent into unknown depths to the right of the green; for the most part the course does not depend on any such dramatic quality, but rather on the combined soundness and subtleness of its architecture. There is a constant demand for accuracy in driving, the more so at present as the rough is really worthy of its name and

the approaches are full of varied interest. In particular, there are one or two holes of the despised length called "drive and pitch" which are entirely fascinating, such as the 5th, with its green almost on the brink of the sea, and the 15th. The greens are full of interesting undulations and altogether I find it hard to imagine a more admirable test of golf.' Times have not changed even over 30 years later. It is still an outstanding course.

The 5th hole almost sank into the sea a few years ago as the Atlantic gales lashed the cliffs but the club's members rallied round and, with outside support,

The ruined Dunluce Castle which gave its name to the championship course at Royal Portrush, where the 1951 Open Championship was played

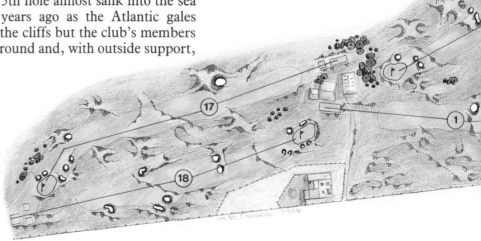

Royal Portrush – Harry Colt's masterpiece

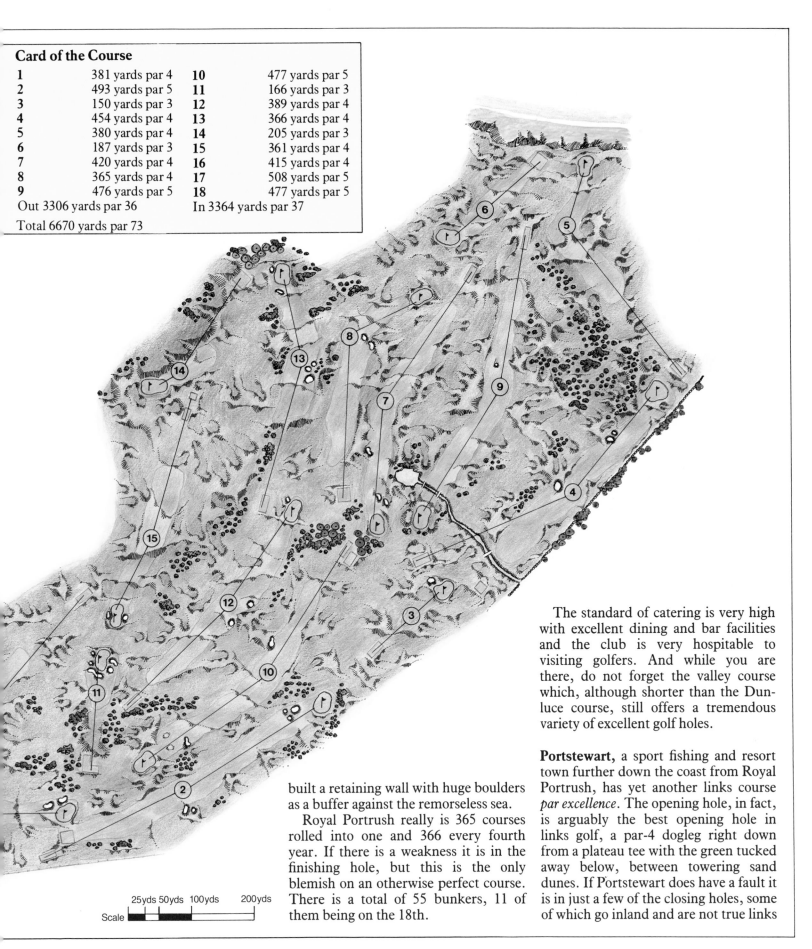

Card of the Course

1	381 yards par 4	10	477 yards par 5
2	493 yards par 5	11	166 yards par 3
3	150 yards par 3	12	389 yards par 4
4	454 yards par 4	13	366 yards par 4
5	380 yards par 4	14	205 yards par 3
6	187 yards par 3	15	361 yards par 4
7	420 yards par 4	16	415 yards par 4
8	365 yards par 4	17	508 yards par 5
9	476 yards par 5	18	477 yards par 5

Out 3306 yards par 36   In 3364 yards par 37

Total 6670 yards par 73

25yds 50yds 100yds 200yds
Scale

built a retaining wall with huge boulders as a buffer against the remorseless sea.

Royal Portrush really is 365 courses rolled into one and 366 every fourth year. If there is a weakness it is in the finishing hole, but this is the only blemish on an otherwise perfect course. There is a total of 55 bunkers, 11 of them being on the 18th.

The standard of catering is very high with excellent dining and bar facilities and the club is very hospitable to visiting golfers. And while you are there, do not forget the valley course which, although shorter than the Dunluce course, still offers a tremendous variety of excellent golf holes.

Portstewart, a sport fishing and resort town further down the coast from Royal Portrush, has yet another links course *par excellence*. The opening hole, in fact, is arguably the best opening hole in links golf, a par-4 dogleg right down from a plateau tee with the green tucked away below, between towering sand dunes. If Portstewart does have a fault it is in just a few of the closing holes, some of which go inland and are not true links

holes. The 16th, for instance, brings the players back to the clubhouse and then they have to drive directly away for the 17th and back parallel for the 18th. This is not the best of situations, especially if it is raining!

However, plans are in hand to build new holes in the dunes beyond the first green and it is hoped that the work will be completed by the time of its centenary in 1994. Although green fees are modest, societies can take advantage of further reductions.

Castlerock with its impressive links course is further along the main A2 coastal road six miles west of Coleraine. The informal atmosphere in the clubhouse ill-prepares you for what is to follow. Far from being an easy relaxing game, this is a case of one challenging hole after another with hardly any let up in concentration or enjoyment.

Ballycastle is the fourth links on the Causeway Coast, along the A2 back past Portstewart, Portrush and the little town of Bushmills with its world-famous whiskey distillery. Together these four courses are the natural setting for any visiting golfer or society.

A magnificent setting for the 5th green at Castlerock – another Irish golfing gem on the Causeway Coast

We have only highlighted the major areas of golf in Northern Ireland. Of course, there are many other courses where you will receive a warm welcome and an enjoyable game of golf. Do not be afraid to try them and discover the natural beauty of the countryside, the spectacular coastline and the high quality of the courses.

Portstewart (left) and Ballycastle (bottom left) are two of the spectacular links courses on Northern Ireland's beautiful Causeway Coast. Enjoy the scenery while you play a challenging round

Bushmills Distillery

No visit to Northern Ireland is complete for a whiskey lover without an outing to Bushmills, the oldest distillery in the world. It is the home of the famous Bushmills Irish Whiskey and the famous 'Black Bush' label. Wherever you go in Northern Ireland, it is everybody's favourite drink.

There are organized tours around the distillery and all visitors are invited to sample a whiskey in the bar. Try a drop of Jimmy Kane's Special – Old Bushmills mixed with water, cloves and cinnamon and served hot – which is sometimes known as a 'hot bush'. For more information on distillery tours, contact Bushmills on (0265) 731521 (tours are Mondays to Thursdays and Friday mornings).

Bushmills Whiskey is linked with the golf world, too. It sponsors the Black Bush Causeway Coast Tournament which is held every year in the first week of June. This is a 72-hole Stableford competition played off handicap on the four spectacular courses of Royal Portrush, Portstewart, Ballycastle and Castlerock. For further details write to the organizer, John Dalzell, at 155 Coleraine Road, Portstewart (Tel. (0265) 832417).

In Ireland you will discover some real golfing gems, whichever area you visit. The popular courses of Ballybunion, Killarney, Waterville, Tralee and Portmarnock are just some of the precious jewels in Ireland's golfing crown. To play on these celebrated courses is a memorable experience, but take time also to discover some of the more remote courses – the ones you have never encountered in your reading or travels. The green fees are often incredibly low, and you

for the winter and the other for the summer, and both are tremendous little tests. The one that backs onto the Liffey is the better of the two but as it was prone to frequent flooding, the other hole was brought into play. The hole has now been moved back and the green raised slightly.

Lucan and **Kilcock** both have nine-hole layouts as you head westwards towards **Knockanally** in County Kildare. Just over 20 miles out of Dublin and only four miles from the village of Prosperous, this fairly open parkland 18-hole layout features an attractive 120-years-old Palladian mansion as the clubhouse. Full catering is available at weekends.

Travelling south through the coun-

The 18th at Royal Dublin: a par-5 that gives the gambler a chance of an eagle if he cuts across the out-of-bounds

try, the N7 is the next big arterial road out of Dublin. It takes you through Ireland's famous 'horse country' with the legendary Curragh racecourse and surrounding stud farms. In fact, the Curragh also refers to a large area of heathland, and within its boundaries is the Irish Republic's oldest golf course.

Curragh Golf Club was formerly a 'Royal' club until the land on which it lies was handed over to the Irish Free State Army in 1922. It has an interesting history and for many years it was believed to have been built well after 1855, the year the nearby military Curragh Camp was established to expand the training requirements for the Crimean War. Now, thanks to Commandant William H. Gibson, a prominent

club member, the true history has been unearthed. A recently found newspaper report from 1942 actually revealed that a match between an Alexander Lowe and a David Ritchie had been played at the links near Donnelly's hollow (a former outdoor boxing arena next to the present-day course) in 1857. Furthermore documents found by Ritchie's granddaughter revealed that he had been a member of Musselburgh and came to Ireland in 1851, laying out the course soon after his arrival – before the army came!

In any event, today the army plays a

The River Liffey flows close by a green at the Hermitage. The course is famous for its superb trees – and good golf, too. It is popular with many Dubliners

big role in the club, forming a sizeable share of the membership. The club's president is always the General Officer Commanding, whether a golfer or not.

Set out in gently contoured heathland, the Curragh, which is a good test, is noted for one or two local hazards. Local farmers have grazing rights which means that you are never alone for long with sheep on the fairways. And when interclub competitions take place many believe that it is more than a coincidence that the nearby army range is often open. Try playing with hand grenades and machine guns going off at the top of your backswing!

Ireland's great golfing discovery, Lillian Behan, who became an international after playing for just two years, is a member here, and for visitors to play on

Close to the port is the peaceful Dun Laoghaire course where a record drive of 392 yards was once hit

help of professional Tommy Halpin, the courses are built on former farmland. But back in 1983, some of the members broke away and formed their own club at Beech Park near Rathcoole in County Dublin. The scenic tree-lined layout is interesting, enjoyable to play and green fees are very low.

Slade Valley's 18 holes are situated high in the Dublin mountains and offer stunning views across five counties. Although they are challenging to your golfing skills, they test your strength and your legs, too, so be warned.

Stackstown and **Dublin Sport** are two more hilly courses to the south of the city. Stackstown was built in 1976 with over 50 per cent of its membership coming from Dublin's Garda (police force). It is tough finding a level lie but the views of Dublin are unbeatable. Dublin Sport has advantages of a different kind – in addition to the golf course, there are a dry ski slope, a swimming pool and hotel. In **Dublin** there are many fine hotels catering for a wide range of budgets. The Tourist Board will be happy to supply you with details (see the address section). Dublin also has its fair share of top restaurants and places of interest if you enjoy sightseeing. Not to be missed is the wonderful Georgian architecture of Fitzwilliam Square. And, of course, it goes without saying that if you really want to get a taste of Dublin and meet the people, you should visit the pubs and try the famous local brew in its home town – Guinness.

the Curragh's 18 holes, the green fees are very reasonable indeed. Three miles away across the race track lies the flat nine-hole course of **Cill Dara**.

Naas has a pleasant nine holes of rolling parkland just off the N7 back towards Dublin, while Four Lakes Golf and Country Club is a new 18-hole parkland course even closer to the city.

Clontarf is the nearest course to the city centre of Dublin. It caters for bowls players as well as golfers and is worth a visit if you play both sports

Bodenstown Golf Club, founded in 1971, is close to the nearby village of Sallins. Owned by entrepreneur Dick Mather, who recently designed the club's second 18-hole course with the

Dublin has many attractive courses on its southside, the majority of which are parkland. They include **Elm Park**, an appealing layout with a stream crossing many of the holes (and tennis, too, if you are a keen player); **Milltown**, an exclusive club which boasts wonderful catering but a fairly flat course; **Castle** which is more undulating and a marginally stiffer test; **Edmondstown; Dun Laoghaire** in a peaceful setting behind the port and the scene of Tommie Campbell's record drive of 392 yards in 1964 when he attempted to bring the par-5 18th to its knees; and **Newlands** to the west.

The Grange lies directly south of the city centre and was established in 1911. James Braid was involved in the original layout, and it is a deceptively tricky and demanding course. Walter Sullivan has been the club's pro for many years and none other than Eamonn Darcy was once a former assistant.

Laid out over mature rolling parkland, it has a gentle introduction with two par-3's opening the card. However, by the time you reach the 18th, the course will have presented you with a formidable test. The 18th itself is a challenging 420 yards requiring an accurate drive downhill to the left opening up an entrance to the green beyond a stream. Green fees are average for Dublin and the clubhouse is very friendly. In such a quiet, peaceful setting, it is difficult to remember that the bustling centre of the city is only a short drive away.

Rathfarnham, Ballinascorney, Killiney and **Carrickmines** are all nine-holers on Dublin's southside. In and around the well-known horse racing track at **Leopardstown** is an 18-hole par-3 cir-

The Grange is quite close to Dublin's centre. James Braid, the course architect, set the golfer some challenging tests as always on this course

cuit plus driving range to complement a full nine-hole course. **Foxrock** is another enjoyable nine-holer with a very amiable club. Set in attractive parkland, John O'Leary started his golf here.

Stepaside, run and funded by the Golf Union of Ireland, gives a marvellous indication of what can be achieved by reclaiming land from a rubbish tip. Designed by Eddie Hackett and landscaped by the council, it is a delightful place and a lesson as to how public courses should be run and built. With special rates for senior citizens, juniors and the unemployed, the basic green fee is very low.

Woodbrook is reached by the main road south from Dublin (the N11). This is yet another of the capital's famous clubs

built close to the town. In 1986 the river that meanders past Bray's second fairway burst its banks in the aftermath of Hurricane Charlie. The result was a few feet of water on the course, and some stranded salmon were left when the waters eventually receded!

Woodenbridge to the south of County Wicklow suffered a similar fate. This picturesque nine-holer was covered in hundreds of tons of silt when the River Avoca decided to look for a new route. However, the members rallied round and cleared the course within days.

Arklow and **Blainroe** are both 18-hole links courses while **Wicklow** has a nine-holer. But for really good holiday golf you need look no further than Delgany and Greystones on the coast 40 minutes' south of Dublin. This area has the proud boast of having produced some of Ireland's finest players including the Bradshaws, Jimmy Martin, Christy Greene, Ray Hayden, Bill Kinsella, Eamonn Darcy and the Dalys. There are numerous hotels, inns and guest houses where you can stay.

Delgany is an attractive, hilly parkland course which was founded in 1908. It is open to visitors at most times and has full catering facilities. The green fees are reasonable and there is a well-stocked pro shop where you can hire clubs if wished.

Greystones is just a couple of miles away and although it is difficult to find, it has all the right ingredients for great holiday golf. With a charming clubhouse, friendly staff and a good course combining some of the best elements of parkland and heath, few visitors leave disappointed. Furthermore, there are great views of the Wicklow Mountains and the Irish Sea, especially from the tee at the 367-yards 18th (the highest point on the course). Try driving the 13th – over 300 yards and uphill all the way.

which has hosted the Carrolls Irish Open. Founded as recently as 1927, the course is a subtle mixture of parkland with a links flavour to some holes. A railway line separates 13 holes close to the sea (the most interesting) from the remaining five. The clubhouse has superb facilities and the course is a popular venue for societies. Green fees are

This view of Greystones gives a good feel of the heath and parkland mix of this pleasant and enjoyable course

slightly on the high side, and visitors are not encouraged to play on Saturdays.

Bray, with its nine-hole course is nearby and there are plans for a new club to be

It is a small club with a big heart and the warmest of welcomes. Green fees are reasonable, too, so make sure you pay it a visit.

From the classic links courses in the north to the scenic parkland layouts in the South, Dublin offers the visitor a feast of golf and at reasonable prices. With so much golf to choose from, wonderful hospitality from the friendly people and an exciting city to discover, Dublin should not be missed.

Dublin is a beautiful city with graceful Georgian buildings and historic churches. Stay there and combine the best of golf with great entertainment, shopping and sightseeing. Some of the sights of Dublin include Christchurch (right), the Merchant's Arch (bottom left), and St Patrick's Cathedral (bottom right)

Waterford glass

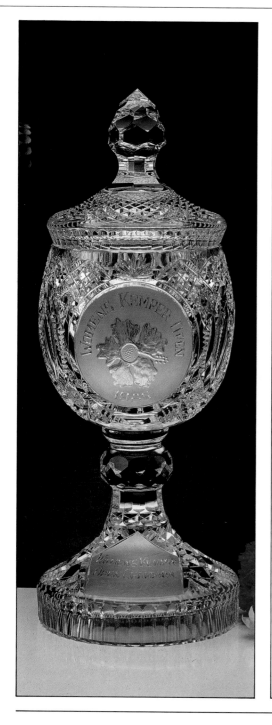

Although Waterford can boast a fine 18-hole golf course, there is no question that the county town is of worldwide renown for its crystal, arguably the finest produced anywhere in the world.

The Waterford Crystal Company does, however, hold strong links with the local golf club, and vice versa. About 80 per cent of the golf membership work at the glass factory, which means that the club is able to host Ireland's biggest annual open golf day, when over £17,000 worth of crystal is put up in prizes. Also, in 1956, Waterford Crystal presented the famous Waterford Scratch Trophy, now one of the most prestigious amateur events in Ireland and Britain. The magnificent trophy, which resides permanently at Waterford Golf Club, took three-and-a-half months to make, stands three feet high and weighs 56lb.

The Waterford Trophy is undoubtedly the showpiece of the crystal company's association with golf. A replica of it adorns the plush, new display room where it stands proudly among other replicas, including the US Tournament Players' Championship, Kemper Open, USF&G Championship, USLPGA Championship, World Championship of Women's Golf, Carrolls Irish Open and Australian Open.

Despite its fame throughout the world, Waterford Crystal did not really become a big name in golf until 1975 when the BBC presented souvenir crystal pieces during the popular Pro-Celebrity TV series at Gleneagles. Bing Crosby, one of the guest celebrities, was so taken with the glass, he started using it as prizes for his own USPGA tournament, the Bing Crosby Pro-Am. From then on, the popularity of the crystal in America grew to such a point that the United States now imports 80 per cent of all the products manufactured at the Waterford factory.

The exceptionally high quality of workmanship that has given Waterford Crystal its tremendous reputation can be witnessed, right from the molten glass stage through to the engravers' room, where the senior cutters are required to have undergone a 10-year apprenticeship. Organized tours are available for visitors and can be booked in advance by phoning the glass factory at Kilbarry on (051) 73311.

Waterford is the only other 18-hole course in the county. This 6323 yards, par-71 parkland layout is the work of Willie Park Jnr. with later modifications by James Braid and Hamilton Stutt. Although there are no apparent problems for the visiting golfer, Waterford is deceptively tough and deserves its reputation as a great inland course.

And a trip to the town could not possibly be complete without a visit to the world-famous Waterford Crystal factory where the renowned Waterford Scratch Trophy, permanently housed at the golf club, was made. Tours of the factory covering every aspect of its manufacturing processes and the chance to buy some beautiful glassware, are available.

The only other two golf courses in County Waterford are the nine-holers at **Dungarvon** and **Lismore**.

Clonmel is a hilly 6349-yards layout just north of the county boundary in County Tipperary. It is a highly enjoyable course which remains largely unknown and unrecognised due to its isolated location which is off the usual tourist beaten track. And you certainly will not have to queue for the first tee here as it rarely gets busy. Once out on the course, you can feel quite alone and isolated, with only the sound of streams babbling down from the mountains and the singing of birds to interrupt the quiet and tranquillity. The layout was designed by the great Irish course architect Eddie Hackett, and it offers a great variety of holes which climb up and down the slopes and hillsides. Accuracy is essential if you are to avoid trees, streams and the odd sprinkling of gorse and heather. Severe slopes also mean that strategic placing of shots will keep the ball from rolling off line.

The three-year-old clubhouse is reminiscent of Switzerland or Austria with its Alpine design and the superb backdrop of pine and fir covered mountains. Full catering is available at lunchtime and dinner for visitors as well as members. Green fees are reasonably priced.

Nenagh and **Thurles** are the two other 18-hole layouts in County Tipperary, both situated in the northern half. Nenagh is a quiet club with a course of only just over 5500 yards and an SSS of 68. Although it may not be much of a challenge to play, it is great exercise for your leg muscles with hills to climb from many of the tees to the greens. No

catering is available.

Thurles is flatter and much busier. Established in 1944, it has nine holes on either side of a main road. It makes a pleasant outing although it is not the most demanding of courses. However, it is advised that you book in advance by phoning the Secretary to be sure of a

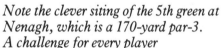

Note the clever siting of the 5th green at Nenagh, which is a 170-yard par-3. A challenge for every player

game.

There are five other courses in Tipperary, but they are all nine-holers, situated at **Carrick-on-Suir, Cahir, Tipperary, Templemore** and **Roscrea**.

The Heath is the only 18-hole course in County Laois (pronounced 'leash'). Situated on common land, it has to share its home with flocks of wandering sheep. However, the 6256 yards, par-71 layout is immensely enjoyable, especially if you manage to avoid some of the immovable hazards that dot the fairways! Most of the course is flat, although the humps and hollows on some holes give the impression of a links layout. Visitors are always welcome in this hospitable club and the catering is excellent. Green fees are reasonable, too, making it well worth a visit.

The neighbouring golf clubs of **Rath-**

The clubhouse at Thurles, flanked by fine trees, is busy and popular

Having knocked the only three mediocre holes on the Old, there is insufficient space to do justice to the rest. Three of those that are justifiably most lauded are the 6th, 9th and 11th. There is not a sand bunker on any of these tremendous par-4's but the second shot to all of them has to be as true as a bullet to hold the target. To err left or right, short or long, is to ensure an exacting piece of wedge practice with absolutely no guarantee of holding the target with the resultant chip shot. The 11th is a particularly heroic hole from the back markers (449 yards) and hardly less stimulating from the ordinary plates at 400 yards. The view from the tee is both magnificent, with the crashing waves not far below, and awesome. A nest of sandhills protects the green as if it were a precious jewel.

The 15th, 16th and 17th (respectively a long par-3 back towards the beach, a par-5 where the green beckons at the far end of a narrow alley between the dunes, and a dogleg left par-4 with a vertigo-inducing tee and Himalayan-like sandhills) bring the round to a tumultuous climax, the 18th being regarded as merely an intriguing walk back to the clubhouse.

Robert Trent Jones seldom had the chance to work on links land. He rejoiced in what he found for his New Course at Bally-bunion. Here are the 4th, 6th and 7th

The smart thing to do on leaving the 17th green is to walk the few yards to the 11th tee on the New. Obviously we cannot advocate that you do that but, nevertheless, one cannot help but ponder what a composite course that would make: holes 1, 2 and 10 to 17 on the Old and 11 to 18 on the New. Since there are many more than 18 great holes in the 36 at Ballybunion this would deny you the privilege of playing gems like the 6th and 7th on the Old or the 4th and 5th on the New, these two being classic examples of the Trent Jones philosophy of easy bogey, tough par. You would also miss out on the 328-yard 10th of which Jones said: "There is no more natural golf hole in the world, an outrageously

The holes through the dunes at Tralee are magnificent. The combination of sea, sand, bays and headlands were the scenic backdrop for 'Ryan's Daughter'

beautiful stretch of God-given terrain." The driving zone is wide enough to be almost visible to the naked eye and the green is at least half the size of Troon's 'Postage Stamp' 8th. In other words, when the wind is against you, it is one of the most difficult par-4's in the world.

The land is magnificent, lending itself to holes like the 13th where it does indeed appear as if the Lord Himself decided on the position of the green. Work only began on the New in the winter of 1981 and the members held the first competition over it in December 1982. It is now in superb condition, and the greens are especially excellent: some of the best putting surfaces you will ever see in the British Isles.

The New owes its existence to the foresight of the club in buying the adjoining land in the 1970s and its development, ironically, has inevitably been assisted by the phenomenal success of the erosion appeal and life

membership scheme launched 10 years ago to help build the defences necessary to safeguard the Old from the ravages of the Atlantic.

Whichever is the better of the two courses, the members at Ballybunion are fortunate to have at their disposal the best 36 holes of links golf anywhere. Visitors are greeted with genuine warmth and a day's golf is worth the high green fees.

Tralee Golf Club is about 40 minutes' drive south of Ballybunion on a finger of land bravely jutting out into the Atlantic Ocean, near the hamlet of Barrow. Tralee is the principal town of County Kerry, but the members of the original golf club were disillusioned with their

marshy nine-holer at Mounthawk which was virtually unplayable during the winter months. So they sold it as a building plot and purchased a property eight miles away at Barrow. The new Tralee was opened in October 1984 at enormous cost. The clubhouse is still a well-equipped Portakabin, and a full programme of bunkering is still in the process of being implemented, but do not let that put you off.

Now assuming that a golf course consists of two elements – its attraction as a place and the quality of the holes themselves – Tralee is another masterpiece. It is impossible to conceive of a more marvellous setting. The course rests upon the steep majestic cliffs made famous in the film *Ryan's Daughter*, and beneath them is a vast expanse of golden sand and a spectacular bay. Across the estuary is the Dingle Peninsula, and the Slieve Mish Mountains dominate the skyline behind you. It is impossible not

to draw comparisons with the beauty of Pebble Beach and Cypress Point. But Peter Dobereiner writes: 'Robert Louis Stevenson was wrong, and by a long chalk, when he described the Monterey Peninsula of California as the finest conjunction of land and sea that this earth has to offer. As a spectacle Tralee is in a different class.'

The course was designed by Arnold Palmer and his indefatigable colleague, Ed Seay. Their plans were approved by the club after a tender competition. There are those in the business who allege that Palmer cannot design a cup and saucer but he has certainly produced a golf course which is a treat to play. He has resisted the urge to go for excessive length. At 5912 metres off the whites and 6210 from the blues it is not

Dooks is one of the oldest courses in Ireland. For many years, little more than rabbits kept the turf cut close until it was later extended to 18 holes

inordinately long and some of the cliff-top holes, especially the long 2nd and short 3rd, are heroic. But like Trent Jones, Palmer was granted a tract of 'God-given terrain' to work with, and one wonders if the 6th, 8th and 15th make the most of the land and whether the generally prosaic inland holes around the clubhouse might be improved.

Tralee is mercilessly exposed to the elements and the wind and salt water have conspired to hamper attempts at nurturing the turf. But the members are a resilient and ambitious bunch and

they will no doubt conquer adversity to bring their course on and erect the clubhouse it deserves. The green fees make a day's golf at Tralee rare value – and remember to take a camera.

Dooks is not on such a grand scale as Tralee but the panorama takes in the peaks of the Kingdom of Kerry and the long promontory of Dingle. To get there, you must follow the Tralee road (the N70) through Killorglin and look for Cromane which is signposted to the right. Turn left at Cromane church and when you see a small bright red building on the right you have arrived, for this is the clubhouse.

Quaint and humble it may look on the outside but inside the clubhouse is a real beauty with an excellent bar. The whole

club has recently undergone a facelift and many improvements have been made.

The club was founded in 1889 with a nine-hole course which was extended to 18 holes in 1970. The turf is half-links, half-meadowland in nature, and the course's status as a sporty holiday test is soon to be upgraded as a result of plans to increase its length, but no doubt idiosyncrasies like the 13th green, which resembles a creased envelope, will be retained.

Considering that there are no permanent greenstaff, the course is in fine condition, totally belying its name (Dooks is the Gaelic word for rabbit warren). Unusually, most of the trouble is behind rather than short of the greens, but Dooks' most singular appeal

Many say that neither of the two Killarney courses are really great golf. But the few other courses that match the setting can be counted on the fingers of one hand

is that it is a haven for the Natterjack Toad. This protected animal features prominently on the club's logo.

Killarney lies approximately the same distance to the other side of Killorglin. This resort offers much more than golf, with fishing and walking being other popular pastimes in this lakeside paradise at the foot of the Macgillicuddy Reeks chain of mountains. Killarney is often claimed by its devotees as the 'Irish Gleneagles' – a claim that is thoroughly justified. It is arguable whether Gleneagles offers marginally

better golf and Killarney better scenery, but they are both top-class courses in beautiful locations.

Golf was introduced to Killarney in 1891 but it was during the 1930s that it enjoyed a renaissance under the supervision of the Viscount Castlerosse, a large man with a large bank account who achieved fame, and presumably notoriety, as the gossip columnist on the *Sunday Express*. Henry Longhurst, the revered golf correspondent of *The Sunday Times*, was one of his closest friends and with his advice and under the direction of Sir Guy Campbell, already established as a course architect of considerable credentials, Castlerosse's dream 18 was laid out around the shores of Lough Leane in this idyllic location.

That masterpiece has since been split

up into two courses: Mahony's Point and Killeen. This move has brought much needed revenue to Killarney over the year but it is aesthetically disappointing. It is probably beyond argument that the best 18 holes at Killarney are the original 18.

The 185-metre, par-3 18th hole at Mahony's Point, which was also the climax to Castlerosse's project, so appealed to Longhurst that he modestly dubbed it "the best short hole in the world". He may have been biased but Frank Pennick, another esteemed architect, was equally complimentary.

There are several great holes other than that gorgeous finale, with the 387-metre 8th at Killeen being as good as any on that course. Like many holes on both layouts it is devoid of sand but not of peril. The overall lure of Killarney was summed up by Pat Ward-Thomas – another late, venerable British golf writer – when he urged that "all golfers should make a pilgrimage to this truly enchanting place".

In conclusion it has to be said that Killarney is maintained in superior

order, and the courses are in perfect shape. The best grasses have been introduced onto the greens and the course is generally as firm as a links. Surprisingly, green fees are not all that expensive, and 18 holes on each course are a must. Do be sure to visit Killarney even if it means making a detour. You cannot help but fall in love with the place.

Waterville lies at almost the southernmost point of Kerry and to reach it the road winds through the glorious scenery of the Ring of Kerry. The course itself measures 7257 yards from the back tees but reduces to 6049 off the 'society' plates. When the wind whips up off the sea, some of the carries can be too demanding for even the strongest hitters in golf.

It is the brainchild of Jack Mulcahy, a wealthy Irish-American. Each July, the Jack Mulcahy Classic is contested there

The Killeen course at Killarney, which followed the original course opened early in World War II, known as Mahony's Point

– a European Tour 'satellite' event. The course itself, designed by Jack and Eddie Hackett, provides a game of two halves. The outward nine is quite ordinary with the exceptions of the 3rd and 4th which are both excellent. However, the homeward half is outstanding bar one or two holes. The 11th, a 477-yard teaser of a par-5 from the middle marker under the deceiving name of 'Tranquillity', may be the best long hole in Ireland. It epitomizes all that is wonderful about Waterville – Birkdale-type

sandhills and a sinuous stretch of immaculately groomed, tumbling fairway winding between the rough grass of the dunes.

The members take particular pride in two short holes on the back nine, the 12th and 17th. The former is 'The Mass Hole', in honour of the priests who used to celebrate the service in the deep hollow in front of the green in the days when praying was a capital offence. The 17th is 'Mulcahy's Peak' because the elevated tee now stands on the spot from

which the boss would survey his site while plotting the routing of the holes. Some purists complain that Mulcahy should have opted for sandy-based links turf rather than deliberately choosing strains of grass more often associated with parkland courses and which inevitably appear a trifle incongruous when set against the proximity of the ocean and the indigenous sandhills. Maybe but it is, after all, Mulcahy's course and any visitor will be grateful that he built it. Green fees, incidentally, are exactly

While he made his money in the United States, Jack Mulcahy dreamed of building a magnificent course on the west coast of Ireland – he did it at Waterville

the same as at Ballybunion, even down to the extra fee for overseas visitors.

If you wish to stay for a few days, the nearby Waterville Lake Hotel has extensive and luxurious facilities and is a great golfing holiday destination.

Lahinch is located further north in County Clare, and only 30 miles north-west of Shannon Airport. The small town overlooks Liscannor Bay and the Cliffs of Moher, and its fabric is inextricably interwoven with the life of the golf club – hence its nickname as the Irish St Andrews. It is another great course and is not eclipsed by the riches of neighbouring Kerry.

The Scots introduced golf to Lahinch in 1893, but it was in 1928 that Dr Alister Mackenzie, who had recently completed work in Cypress Point and was soon afterwards to build Augusta National in collaboration with Bobby Jones, revised the links. He eventually left the job contented with what he had done. "Lahinch will make the finest and most popular course that I, or I believe anyone else, ever constructed", he said. Although that has to be an overstatement of Lahinch's worth, it does indicate the calibre of the place, and Mackenzie was demonstrably not a man whose opinion can be easily ignored.

Good golf holes abound at Lahinch.

A view up in the dunes at Lahinch, with the ruined O'Brien's Castle in the distance

Some of the par-4s utilize the fabulous terrain to absolutely optimum advantage. The stretch from the 7th to the 10th is especially memorable in this respect. Two holes that Mackenzie was not permitted to touch were the 5th and 6th, a long hole and a short one, respectively known as 'Klondyke' and 'Dell'. The former measures 453 metres

and the second shot has to clear a central mound very much in the fashion of the 16th hole at Southport & Ainsdale. The 6th is that ultimate horror, a blind par-3, where the only clue as to the direction of the flag is a white stone which is shifted every time a new cup is cut. These two holes are anachronisms, but not without charm unless you have run up a double-bogey.

Like Killarney, the course has been subject to a few modifications, notably the adding of new tees at the 9th and 13th and the moving back of the greens on the 7th and 12th. This has primarily been done according to plans drawn up by Donald Steel. And if competitors baulk at the prospect of playing the 'Dell', the club could always use its genuine 19th hole; a fine new par-3 inserted between the 8th and 9th in case of emergencies.

The South of Ireland Amateur Championship was inaugurated at Lahinch in 1895 and the club has remained the permanent home to this prestigious event. It is played over the Cham-

Most golfers reckon that the holes running close to the Atlantic are the best at Waterville – superb golfing country

pionship Course, to which one is always referring when talking of Lahinch. There is also a short holiday 18, the Castle Course, across the road, encircling the solitary tower of O'Brien's Castle.

Green fees are lower, of course, on the Castle Course but even on the Championship one they are not unreasonable, although higher at weekends and on bank holidays.

Shannon Golf Club is close to the international airport and the River Shannon's estuary. This excellent inland course was laid out by John Harris and, in common with all the courses in the region, it is open 12 months of the year. However, because it is so close to the river, it can suffer in the wake of a long wet spell. On such occasions its 6900 yards plays uncomfortably longer than suggested by the card. Green fees are reasonably priced and it is the pick of the remaining three 18-hole courses and four nine-holers in County Clare.

Cork Golf Club, overlooking the town's harbour on Little Island, lies south of Clare and east of Kerry. Cork is the largest county in Ireland. Not only is it

an area of outstanding beauty and history but it also has 19 golf courses.

The present site was found only after four previous removals. Cork was another course worked upon by Alister Mackenzie in the 1920s and he combined an old quarry and the undulating terrain to characteristically splendid effect. The greens are large but always in fine fettle and the members can boast an impressive pedigree of important tournaments, both professional and amateur. A round at Little Island concludes with a severe five-hole examination of tough par-4's but perhaps the 455-yard 4th is the best of the bunch. It is a classic of the 'he who dares' genre. The more of the carry across the hazard you are able to chew off, the more chance there is of reaching the green in two.

Little Island's most famous son was Jimmy Bruen. His portrait adorns the

The 9th tee at Cork. The course looks at its very best when the huge clumps of golden gorse are in bloom

clubhouse lounge, a tribute to a fellow who as a young man was in the victorious Walker Cup team against the Americans at St Andrews in 1938 and later, in 1946, was the British Amateur Champion.

Douglas Golf Club lies on a hillside above the city of Cork. At 6131 yards it is 500 yards shorter than nearby Cork but is possesses picturesque views also – over Cork itself and out to the surrounding countryside. **Monkstown** and **Muskerry** are two other courses in the immediate vicinity. The former was extended to 18 holes in 1970 while the latter, seven miles to the north-west of Cork, is a riot of colour when the furze is in bloom. The River Shournagh

comes devilishly into play on the 429-yard 17th. Muskerry is situated less than two miles from the world-famous Blarney Castle which is an obvious detour if you fancy kissing the world-famous Blarney Stone for luck and conversational prowess!

Mallow, 21 miles north of Cork city, is unusual among Irish golf clubs in that it also offers squash, tennis, an indoor games room and a sauna. The golf course is an exacting test of nearly 6800 yards and is widely considered to be the best course in the county outside the city itself. There are five other 18-hole layouts in County Cork at **Bandon, Charleville, East Cork, Fermoy** and **Youghal**. The shorter courses of **Kanturk** and **Macroom** have alternative tees so that their nine holes present the visitor with a slightly different challenge on the second circuit.

most scenic holes to be encountered anywhere. The 580 yards 15th bends around the edge of Clew Bay after a very intimidating drive over an inlet which tends to get wider with every glance. Anyone securing a par from the back tee can feel proud of a job well done.

Because of its slightly remote location Westport's membership is fairly widespread and so the club is only really busy at weekends when visitors are recommended to call up in advance. Full catering is available, although it is better to order your meal before playing to avoid delays, and the low green fees are an undoubted bargain for a course of this class.

Castlebar is only a short drive from Westport and its gently rolling parkland course is welcome relaxation if you are still feeling shell-shocked from the

The view from the tee at the 580-yard 15th at Westport. The carry is not enormous – at least, not until the wind is blowing straight at you

rigours of the former. A comfortable length at 6100 yards, this former holiday home of the late British prime minister Clement Attlee is not too much of a strain for the average player and is only really busy at weekends. Bar snacks are available in the clubhouse, and green fees are low in keeping with other courses in the area.

Inniscrone is set on the shores of Killala Bay and is the home of one of the hidden gems of the north-west. It has been discovered by the fortunate few who return every year, including former 'James Bond', Sean Connery.

Laid out on classic links terrain the

course has all the normal characteristics of sea-side golf – sand dunes, humps and hollows, thick rough and lightning-fast greens. It is a real joy for anyone who enjoys playing golf as near as possible to the way it was in days gone by. The best holes are found at the far end, around the turn. The 7th, known as 'Hogs Back', is appropriately named as the fairway slopes sharply away on either side, while the short 8th is a gem of a hole where the premium is again on accuracy. Pride of place, however, must go to the 9th and 10th, par 4's which would not look out of place on the best of courses. Neither is very long – the 9th is 357 yards and the 10th even shorter at 338 – but the opportunities for disaster are plentiful, the penalties for missing either fairway or green being exceptionally harsh. This is certainly a course not to be missed and as the club is very keen to encourage visitors, a warm welcome is assured. Green fees are reasonable, and married couples can play together very economically indeed.

Rosses Point, a little further along the coast near the pretty town of Sligo, is the home of County Sligo Golf Club, and is undoubtedly the best course in this part of the Republic. For many years, it has played host to the West of Ireland Championship. The beautiful links is blessed with that wonderful turf found only by the sea, and offers superb panoramic views across Donegal Bay. In fact, from the 9th tee, it is possible to

The beautifully sited 10th green at Enniscrone (right) and the 17th at Rosses Point (below) which many of the club's members consider to be the best hole and the most difficult on the course

Every course on the west coast of Ireland seems to have a magnificent setting. This is another scene at Rosses Point

facing an almost certain three putts.

You might expect that the green fees would be set at a discouraging level for a course of this superior standard, but at Rosses Point this is not the case. A weekday round is still very reasonable with only a small premium at weekends. For golfing addicts who cannot drag themselves away, there is even a special monthly bargain price which may prove irresistible. Only the remoteness of the course prevents the inclusion of Rosses Point in the British *Golf World* magazine's top 50 courses in the British Isles. Peter Alliss said of the course: "I did think Rosses Point was a gentle sleeping giant and something people should go and look at and I think they will come away marvelling at its beauty. The great test of any golf course is that it can be a tremendous test for the highest quality player and great fun for the modest competitor, and that is where Ross Point has got it made. I have never visited the course before but had heard a lot about Ballybunion, Tralee, Connemara and Lahinch, but Rosses Point stands at the very top of the list of Irish courses, and it is one more people should discover."

Bundoran lies further north along the coastal road from Rosses Point through the narrow neck which connects Donegal with the rest of the Republic. Founded in 1894, this fairly exposed links course was altered in the 1930s by six-times Open Champion Harry Vardon. It is owned by the local hotel which leases the course to the club. Hotel guests play for free, but the green fees are still modest for other visitors.

For seven years in the 1950s, Bundoran was home to the legendary Christy O'Connor who is still remembered fondly by the locals. Catering is available in the hotel, and generally there is no need to book ahead for a game on a course which is good enough to have hosted the Irish Professional Championship in the past.

see five counties – Sligo, Donegal, Roscommon, Leitrim and Mayo.

It is difficult to select the best hole on the course, there being so many candidates, but the 8th, a classic par-4, takes some beating. Two perfect shots around the dogleg are required if the hidden burn is to be avoided and a birdie-putt

Christy O'Connor enjoyed many tournament successes when he was the professional at Bundoran in the 1950s

to result. The ferociously difficult 17th with its steeply sloping putting surface is another memorable test. Any player finding himself above the hole here is

Donegal is the next stop up the N15 road, and if you are intending to play over the local course, you must be careful not to miss the signposts to the club as you approach the town. In fact, it is five miles outside at Murvagh and easily missed if you are driving fast. This is another relatively new course which was opened in 1976. Designed by the ubiquitous Eddie Hackett, the course must be one of the most severe tests of golf and examinations of skill to be found anywhere. Indeed, it is Donegal's proud boast that off the back tees the course is the longest in the British Isles, measuring over 7200 yards.

Exposed to the elements and isolated from the rest of the world, it is a mixture of both inland and links-type terrain with many good holes, but the short 5th will not be forgotten easily by any visitor. Green fees are reasonable and you should not have to book.

Donegal (top) is a part links, part inland golf course. The view shown here is of the 7th green in links country

The sweep of the bay at Tra na Rosann in County Donegal (above). The Donegal coastline has many fine beaches

The many splendours of Donegal, a county that combines rugged mountain scenery with a beautiful coastline. You can view the natural beauty of Glengesh (1), see typical cottages (2), visit Glenveagh National Park (3), or the Errigal Mountains (4). Or you can just enjoy the majestic beaches and cliff walks, as shown here near Kilcar (5)

Letterkenny is another Eddie Hackett-designed course and it was opened in 1968. It is an attractive, holiday-type course overlooking Lough Swilly. Not too difficult for even higher handicappers, with very generous fairways and nothing much in the way of rough, it is perfect for a nice soothing round of golf, especially if you have played at Inniscrone, Rosses Point and Donegal and are feeling in need of a slight break. The more interesting holes in Letterkenny are to be found on the hill around the

The beautiful Lough Swilly (right) is close to Letterkenny golf course. The course is set partly on a hill and partly on the flat. The 18th hole (below) is a good par-5 which plays gently downhill

clubhouse area, the lower half down by the Lough being on very flat ground, and the 18th is indicative of this. It is a very attractive downhill par-5 with potential disaster lurking both left and right – a great finishing hole and a real test for anyone 'protecting' a score. Visitors are welcome here at any time, green fees are low and bar snacks are available in the extremely attractive clubhouse.

Rosapenna stands on the western side of Lough Swilly which splits the top half of Donegal in two. The original course was laid out by Old Tom Morris and opened in 1893, but the design was altered in 1906 by Harry Vardon and James Braid. The barren windswept links overlook Sheephaven Bay and

there are some fine holes, particularly those following the line of the beach. The good sandy soil enables the course to stay open all the year round, even though the hotel that owns it is closed between October and Easter. Green fees are low and if you enjoy battling with the wind and like your golf 'in the raw', you will be in your element here.

Portsalon Golf Club, founded in 1897, was one of the four founder members of the Golfing Union of Ireland along with Royal Portrush, Royal County Down and Royal Dublin. Unfortunately, because it really is a wonderful setting and still has enormous potential, the course,

The superbly natural course at Rosapenna: no earth-moving equipment was used here

unlike its illustrious partners, has, due to lack of funds, suffered from some neglect over the years. However, the club, which only has 80 members, has recently purchased the course and improvements, combined with proper maintenance, are top of the agenda. Portsalon really is a wonderful place to play and certainly not expensive. Do not let first impressions put you off – there are some great holes out there, and do not be misled by some rather mysterious tee-boxes!

Also, because the club has no clubhouse, visitors are required to pay their green fee at Rita's Bar, a small shop-cum-pub about 300 yards from the 1st tee. A course not to be missed, if only for the wonderful views and the completion of your golfing education.

The 3rd green at Portsalon. The club has very few members so this is the ideal course for a quiet and relaxing day out

Narin and Portnoo, about one hour's drive west of Letterkenny, is another course suffering from lack of exposure due entirely to its rather remote location. Opened as long ago as 1930, it is a deceptively difficult little links with greens that make elusive targets, exacting severe penalties for even the narrowest miss. It is very old-fashioned in nature, like a cross between Prestwick and North Berwick, both the ultimate in leave-it-as-you-find-it seaside courses. Although it is easy to become rather blasé after a while about the scenery in this part of the world, the views from the far end of the course do not let the rest of Donegal down. They are simply spectacular, as are the greens – a pleasure both to look at and to putt on.

Societies are not allowed to play at Narin and Portnoo in June, July and August because the course is very busy with the influx of holidaying country members staying in the many and varied summer homes overlooking the 1st tee. Casual visitors can pay for a round, but it is advisable to call up beforehand.

Ballybofey and Stranorlar is a compact little course south from Letterkenny and split down the middle by the N56 road. The parkland layout has small well-kept greens which are deceptively difficult to hit and hold. The most scenic hole is the 8th where the tee is set out on Loch Alan – a nerve-racking shot for the most experienced golfer. Extended to 18 holes in 1979, it is a pleasant place to play and not too demanding. However, it is sufficiently interesting to capture your complete attention and is very economical for a day's play.

Carrick-on-Shannon, Boyle, Castlerea and **Roscommon** are a convenient cluster of nine-holers in the counties of Leitrim and Roscommon. Although they are all relatively undemanding in nature, they are worth a visit if you are passing through the area. The best is probably Roscommon which has the distinction of being a nine-hole course

Tumbling ground at Narin and Portnoo. Probably the original club members just chose natural sites for greens and tees and began playing. This is the 10th hole

with 11 greens and 14 tees. It also has a very strong junior section which produced the 1986 Irish Boys' and Girls' Champions.

There is a superb beach at Narin (1) as well as a golf course. While you are staying in the region, you could visit the ruins of Roscommon Abbey (2). If money is no object and you have always wanted to stay in a real castle, you could enjoy the luxurious splendours of Ashford Castle Hotel at Cong in County Mayo (3)

Like all the other areas of Ireland, both in the Republic and the North, the clubs in this area were remarkably hospitable and it is difficult to envisage a more enthusiastic and knowledgeable group of people than you will encounter here. There are plenty of friendly hotels, guest houses and bed-and-breakfast establishments where you can stay and it is easy to plan a hugely enjoyable golfing itinerary that takes in a wide range of courses – inland and links; demanding and relaxing; Championship and little-known. As in Scotland, golf in Ireland is still the game of the people and they will want to share it with you wherever you go.

1

2

3

Discovering beautiful Ireland

*I*reland is a marvellous place for a holiday and offers you a wide range of sports, activities and sightseeing. In addition to playing golf you can enjoy the trout and salmon fishing, horse-riding, swimming and watersports, bowls and tennis. Many of the larger hotels and even some golf clubs have their own sports facilities. Ireland is a country of outstanding beauty with a spectacular coastline, wild and rugged mountains and national parks, and astonishingly green hills and meadows. The beaches are relatively uncrowded even in high summer.

There is more than golf to Ireland and while you are staying there, you should explore the country and see some magnificent places – the Killarney Lakes (1), the Dartry mountains in County Sligo (2) and the holy sites of Kilfenora (3) and Glendalough (4), for instance